WORLD IN VIEW

WALES

Kath Davies

M
MACMILLAN

First published 1990

Published by
Macmillan Children's Books
A division of
MACMILLAN PUBLISHERS LTD
Houndmills, Basingstoke, Hampshire RG21 2XS
and London
Companies and representatives
throughout the world

Designed by Julian Holland Publishing Ltd
Picture research by Jennifer Johnson

Printed in Hong Kong

British Library Cataloguing in Publication Data
Davies, Kath
Wales.
1. Wales
I. Title II. Series
942.9085'8

ISBN 0-333-48644-7

Photographic credits: cover: Spectrum, title page,5, 8 Celtic Picture Agency, 9 AA Picture Library, 10 Celtic Picture Agency, 11 M J Thomas/Celtic Picture Agency, 15 AA Picture Library, 16 Ray Mitchell/Celtic Picture Agency, 17 AA Picture Library, 19 Celtic Picture Agency, 21 Rex Features, 24 Mary Evans Picture Library, 27 Popperfoto, 28 M J Thomas/Celtic Picture Agency, 29 Barry Webb/Celtic Picture Agency, 30 Plaid Cymru, 33 M J Thomas/Celtic Picture Agency, 34 Celtic Picture Agency, 37 Mary Evans Picture Library, 39 M J Thomas/Celtic Picture Agency, 41 Celtic Picture Agency, 43, 44 M J Thomas/Celtic Picture Agency, 45 J Draddy/Celtic Picture Agency, 49 Rudy Lewis/Celtic Picture Agency, 51 M J Thomas/Celtic Picture Agency, 52 AA Picture Library, 54 Rudy Lewis/Celtic Picture Agency, 55 M J Thomas/Celtic Picture Agency, 57 British Coal, 58 Jack Hartley/Celtic Picture Agency, 61 Celtic Picture Agency, 63 M J Thomas/Celtic Picture Agency, 65 Celtic Picture Agency, 67 AA Picture Library, 69 M J Thomas/Celtic Picture Agency, 71 Colin Johnson, 75 Rudy Lewis/Celtic Picture Agency, 78 British Coal, 80 Rudy Lewis/Celtic Picture Agency, 81 M J Thomas/Celtic Picture Agency, 84 Kath Davies, 88 Paul Evans, 89 The Bridgeman Art Library, 92, 93 M J Thomas/Celtic Picture Agency.

Cover: *Conwy Castle, Gwynedd*
Title page: *Big Pit, now a mining museum*

Contents

Red Dragon of Wales

1 Introducing Wales

Wales, called *Cymru* in Welsh, is a land of mountains and river valleys, hills and streams. The lakes and moors of the uplands contrast sharply with the cliffs and sandy estuaries of its jagged coastline.

Almost all the rock that makes up Wales is more than 200 million years old. In some parts of the island of Anglesey the rock is even older, going back more than 650 million years. Cambrian, Ordovician and Silurian rocks, which are among the oldest rocks in the world, are called after either the Roman name for Wales itself, which was Cambria, or after groups of people who lived there in the past.

Most of Wales is bordered by the sea. It has a spectacular coastline with huge cliffs and large sandy bays, such as this one at Three Cliffs Bay on the Gower Peninsula. This area is very popular with tourists.

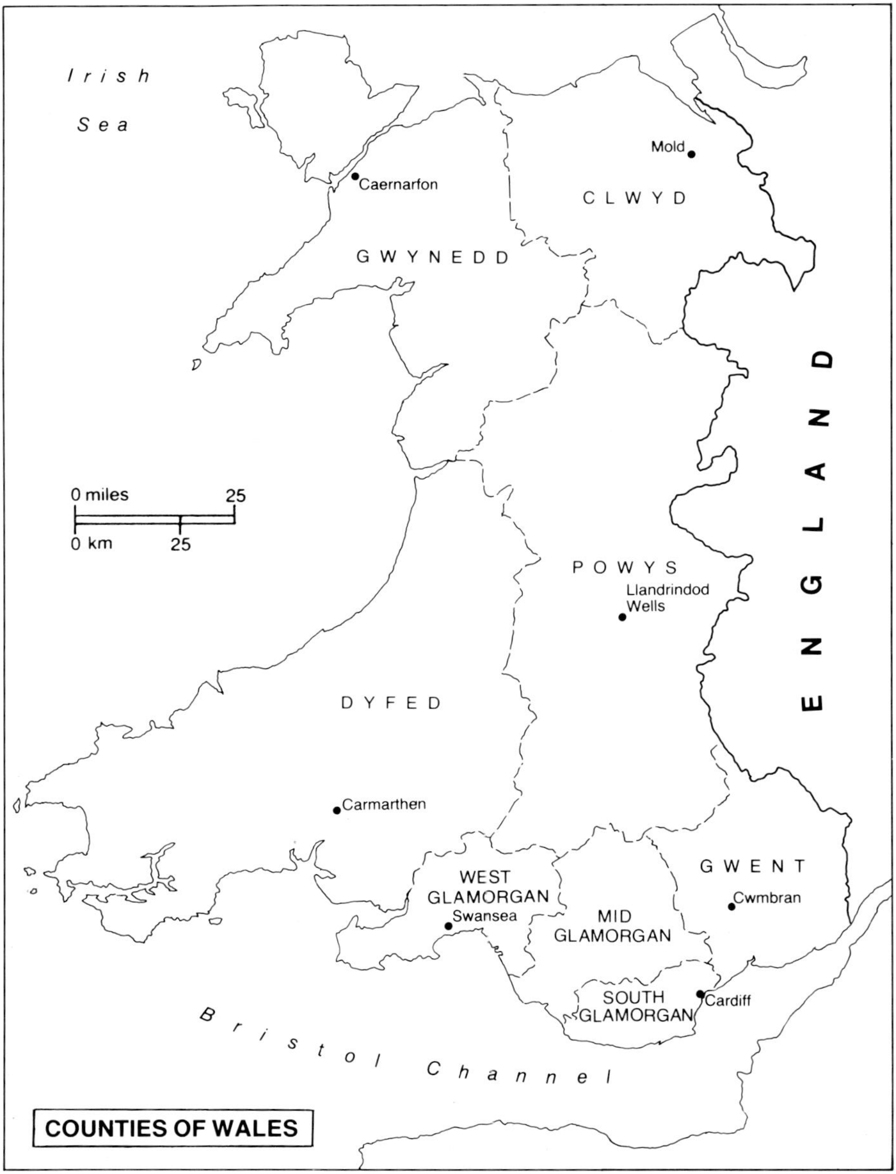

COUNTIES OF WALES

Wales' only land border lies to the east, where it joins England. To the north and west its border is the Irish Sea, to the south the Bristol Channel, and to the south-west the Celtic Sea. The island of Anglesey, *Ynys Mon,* lies off the mainland region of Gwynedd in North Wales, across the narrow Menai Strait.

Wales is the smallest of the countries in the British Isles, which lie at the western edge of the continent of Europe. Its land area of just over 20 720 square kilometres (8000 square miles) is half the size of Switzerland, or about the same size as the North American state of Massachusetts. Yet within that small country many different landscapes may be found, and North, Mid- and South Wales are all quite different from one another. In the north there are high mountains, with crags and peaks, contrasting with the rolling, more gentle hills of Mid-Wales. In the south, the wide plains of the Tywi estuary and the coastal farmlands seem like almost another country.

Mountain and lowland

About one quarter of Wales lies above 305 metres (1000 feet).The mountains rise from the Brecon Beacons in the south to the peaks of Snowdonia, *Eryri,* in the north. Snowdon, *Yr Wyddf,* is the highest of these peaks, and at 1085 metres (3560 feet) it is the highest mountain in Wales and England. The Cambrian Mountains stretch from the Clwydian range in the north-east to the barren hills of the Preseli in the south-west. Moorland and mountains form the central core of Wales.

Most of the low-lying land in Wales is found around the coast and along the river valleys. The

Much of Wales was covered by ice during the Ice Age and there are many valleys which have been scoured out by glaciers. This typical glacial valley, viewed from Nant Ffrancon Pass, clearly shows the U-shape that glaciers leave behind.

coastal plains of the north and the Vale of Glamorgan through the Gower into Dyfed have always provided fertile land for farming. Rivers in Wales are like the spokes of a wheel, flowing out from the centre of the country to its coast. The Severn, the Wye and the Usk all rise in the uplands of Mid-Wales and end at the south coast. In the north, the Conwy, the Clwyd and the Dee flow from the mountains to the Irish Sea. The Dee reaches the sea through a wide flat estuary south-west of the Wirral peninsula.

Using the land

Most of Wales is not suitable for growing crops. The climate in upland areas is wet and windy, and the soil is poor. Coarse grass, gorse, moss and bracken grow there, and the land is used for rough grazing for sheep farms. Heather grows where there are no sheep.

In some areas large numbers of trees have been planted by the Forestry Commission which now looks after about eight per cent of all the forests in Wales.

Crops are grown successfully in the valleys of the Conwy and Clwyd, and in Glamorgan and the border country. Anglesey also grows crops, mainly cereals. It used to be called *Mam Cymru*, the mother of Wales, because the crops grown there were used to feed people on the mainland. Dairy farming is also found in lowland areas of Wales such as the northern Vale of Clwyd and Dyfed in the south-west.

Coal, iron and slate have been found in some of the southern valleys and the harsher upland areas

Unlike the mountain areas, which are mostly moorland, the gentle rolling landscape of the valley of the Tywi River, in the south, is fertile enough to be used for growing crops as well as rearing cows and sheep.

of the north. Industries grew up around these deposits, changing the appearance of the landscape over the last 200 years. These industries have had far-reaching effects not only on the economy of the country but also on Welsh people's lives.

The high peaks of Snowdonia cause the clouds moving in from the Atlantic Ocean to drop plenty of rain. This cascades down the mountains and valleys to form waterfalls and lakes such as Llynnau Mymbyr. Many youth groups come from all over England and Wales to use the lakes and rivers for canoeing.

Climate

Very hot summers or very cold winters are unusual in Wales which has a mild climate without harsh extremes. The temperature is generally cool. The west coast has high winds but mild winters, while the eastern lowlands are more misty, with fog in autumn and winter.

The rainfall in Wales is probably its most marked feature. Snowdonia has about 4000 millimetres (157.5 inches) of rain every year, and

There are many parts of Wales where the land has been scarred by quarrying slate or mining coal. The sides of this mountain in Gwynedd have been gouged away by the Penrhyn slate quarry, leaving huge heaps of spoil, or slag, to loom over the village of Bethesda.

the north coast and the borders experience about 750 millimetres (29.5 inches). Many parts of the country receive about 1250 millimetres (49.2 inches). It is sunniest in May and June and wettest in July and August, but in Wales the weather is always changing. Most of the country has about 1500 hours of sunshine every year, but in the mountain areas the amount of sunshine drops to around 1200 hours. Some areas away from high ground, such as Anglesey, may have as many as 1600 hours of sunshine.

Natural resources

The natural resources found in Wales have shaped both the landscape and the lives of the people. Stone walls mark the edges of fields and stone buildings are to be seen everywhere. Slate, found in the mountains of Snowdonia, has provided roofs for buildings all over the world. In Wales, especially in the north, slate has also been used to make everything from fenceposts to tombstones, decorated fireplaces and even ornaments.

Coal and iron mining as well as tinplate and steel working in the south have given a distinctive look to the industrial towns of the valleys such as Ebbw Vale or the Rhondda. Lead was mined in the north and in north Dyfed, and copper in Anglesey. Small amounts of gold and silver were also found in Mid-Wales. A number of these metal mines are no longer worked today, but they have been converted into museums showing what life was like for the people who once worked there.

In the south, the once scarred valleys of the coal mines are gradually becoming green once more now that many of the pits have closed. In the north, some of the slate tips have been landscaped and turned into parks.

2 From the Celts to nationalism

Throughout their history, Welsh people have been fighting off invaders. Some came from the east over land, and others from the west by sea. Romans, Saxons, Vikings and Normans each in their turn threatened the people who lived in what is now called Wales. Last of all, and most lasting, came the English.

The first people came to Wales from Europe between 50 000 and 10 000 years ago. They lived by hunting and gathering food. Then, between 10 000 and 3000 years ago, more people came from Europe. They brought new farming methods with them, and the skills of stone and metal working. Archaeologists think that this wave of people may have been small and dark-haired, and could have been amongst the ancestors of Welsh people today.

The Celts

The first people who may be thought of as distinctly Welsh came to Wales in the Celtic Iron Age, about 3000 years ago. The Celts were warriors, both women and men. Originally from central Europe, they had settled in most of western Europe by about 1500 years ago. The Celts were a well-organized people. They lived in groups of families and their rulers included the Druids, who were priests and lawmakers. The Druids also kept tribes in touch with one another.

The Celts built fences or walls around their

homes to keep enemies and animals out. They also built hill forts, where they may have lived in times of war. They kept some animals and grew crops, and they were skilled metalworkers. The jewellery, weapons and household objects which have been found from those distant days are decorated with birds, beasts and the strange, laced designs now called Celtic patterning.

Celtic culture has survived in Wales, Scotland, Ireland, the Isle of Man, Cornwall and Brittany. The language, literature, folklore and legends of these countries, as well as some of the objects that have been found, show a direct link stretching back from the present into the Celtic past.

Roman invaders

The Celts dominated Wales until the Romans invaded. By AD78 the Romans had overcome the Celtic leader Caradog and crushed the power of the Druids at a battle in Anglesey. Once in control, they built forts such as Segontium (Caernarfon) in the north and Isca (Caerleon) in the south, and roads to link their towns and forts. Roman roads and the remains of their forts can still be seen in Wales today.

The Romans grew crops to feed their armies and their empire, and they mined metals such as lead, gold and silver. Latin was the language of Rome, and some Welsh words show traces of Latin influence. Roman rule in Wales lasted almost 400 years. During that time Christianity was introduced into Britain and into Wales, though many Celtic people continued to worship their own goddesses and gods.

In the fifth and sixth centuries, centres of

The early settlers in Wales have left behind important remains. At Din Lligwy on the island of Anglesey there are the ruins of a settlement made of circular stone huts. The settlement is dated about AD400.

Christian learning were established in places such as LlanIlltud Fawr (Llantwit Major) in South Wales. Amongst the preachers and teachers who set out to bring Christianity to the people was Dewi (David), patron saint of Wales, who founded a monastery in Dyfed.

At this time, there were well-used sea routes between West Wales and Ireland, Cornwall and Brittany. There were settlements of Irish Celts in North and West Wales. They may have been driven out of Wales by a Celtic tribe from the north of Britain, the Gododdyn, led by Cunedda. He conquered, then gave his name to, Gwynedd.

The Romans quickly established dominance over southern England and Wales, and were able to build large fortresses. The fortress at Isca Silurum, now called Caerleon, was large enough to have a circus built for fights with gladiators and other entertainments. The site has been excavated and is now a tourist attraction.

Saxons and Vikings

When the Saxons invaded, they cut off the Celts of the north and south-west of Britain from the Celts in Wales. The invaders' name for the Celts was *Wealas,* meaning the Welsh, or foreigners. The Welsh called themselves *y Cymry* which means comrades or people of the same country. The first distinct eastern border to the country of the Welsh was Offa's Dyke. King Offa built the dyke about 784 to mark out the border of his own kingdom of Mercia, and in doing so he made a boundary that can still be seen today. The border between England and Wales still follows parts of Offa's Dyke.

There were Viking raids on the coasts and into some river valleys during the ninth century, but they left their influence on the landscape only in a few place names such as Skomer, Solvo and Skokholm in the south-west.

By the tenth century, Wales had its own laws, language and customs, and had become a land of small principalities, each with its own ruler. The provinces all had some independence, but had links with one another.

When Offa became king of the southern part of England known as Mercia, he built a defensive ditch and wall along the boundary of Mercia and Wales. This ditch, or dyke, can be clearly seen along parts of the present Welsh border.

Early organization of Wales
One of the princes, known as Hywel Dda, (Hywel the Good) was responsible for setting out the laws of Wales. The way this was done showed very clearly how society was organized in Wales at that time.

Gwlad – the country
Cantref – the province
Cwmwd – the district
Tref – the village

There were two main groups of people: those who were free and those who were not. The highest ruler was the *brenin,* or prince, and the *uchelwyr* were the landowners or aristocracy. The *aillt* or *teog* were people who were part of the extended family or servant class. They had some freedom, but the *caethwas,* had no independence whatsoever.

Families seem to have been responsible for looking after all their members. When a land holder died, for example, the property was divided amongst the children. This system was called gavelkind. In the system used elsewhere, called primogeniture, the eldest child inherited everything.

The Norman conquest

After the Normans had conquered England in 1066, William of Normandy set three of his most powerful barons on the Welsh borders at Chester, Shrewsbury and Hereford. He gave them a free hand to subdue Wales. As the Normans advanced, they built castles to maintain their position. They also made treaties with some Welsh rulers as they went, so that new loyalties were formed. The Welsh did not organize themselves strongly enough to resist this new invader, and by the twelfth century most of the lowlands had come under Norman influence. Only Gwynedd in the north held out.

A bid for freedom

During the twelfth and thirteenth centuries Wales was protected by the building of large castles. Pembroke Castle was built in about 1200, to guard the entrance to Wales in the safe harbour of Milford Haven. Pembroke Castle was the birth place of Henry Tudor who, as Henry VII, united England and Wales.

During the 100 years between 1173 and 1282 Wales was almost united against the threat from across the border. Two princes of Gwynedd, Llywelyn Fawr (the Great) and Llywelyn 'Ein Lyw Olas', Our Last Leader, succeeded in bringing most of the Welsh lands under their rule. Llywelyn Fawr was acknowledged by the other Welsh rulers as prince or overlord. The English king, Henry III made treaties with Llywelyn the

Last that allowed them both to exist in peace.

These peace-making attempts soon failed. In 1282, Edward I of England invaded Wales with superior military strength and Llywelyn and his brother David were both killed. From 1284, Wales became a principality of England. Edward built a series of massive castles along the Welsh border and in places such as Caernarfon and Beaumaris in the north. His son, also Edward, was given the title of Prince of Wales, and since that time the eldest son of the monarch has held the title. The first English Prince of Wales was invested with the title at Caernarfon, 700 years ago.

In 1969, Prince Charles, the eldest son of Queen Elizabeth II, was invested as Prince of Wales at Caernarfon Castle. The elaborate ceremony was a sign of the status of Wales as a separate principality.

Owain Glyndŵr

The last attempt to raise the Welsh against the English was made between 1400 and 1405 by a prince from Mid-Wales, Owain Glyndŵr. Owain was descended from all three Welsh princedoms, so he could command the loyalty of many Welsh people who were unhappy with English rule. His campaign began in North Wales, and he succeeded in calling a parliament at Machynlleth. The building where it took place can still be seen.

Glyndŵr's attempt did not succeed. He himself disappeared and no one knows how or when he died. Today, he is part of the legend and folklore of Wales. After Glyndŵr's failure Welsh people lost many of their rights. By law they were no longer allowed to hold public meetings nor to hold any public position. They could not acquire land, bear arms, or be citizens of border towns, nor could they take part in a trial of an English person. Englishmen who married Welsh women lost their rights in the same way.

3 The rise of nationalism

In 1485, a Welshman, Henry Tudor, won the English crown in battle and became Henry VII. Many Welsh people thought that Henry would now put right the wrongs of the previous ages. However, although Henry gave high positions at court to many of his Welsh supporters, he did nothing to help Wales as a country. Some Welsh rights were reinstated and at the same time laws were passed which seemed to give Welsh people equality with the English. In fact these new laws had the effect of destroying much of what remained of Welsh life.

In 1536 and 1543 Wales finally came under English rule by law. The Acts of Union replaced the laws dating from the time of Hywel Dda with English law. The Welsh landowners from this time on began to be identified with the English upper classes, and the gap between them and the ordinary people of Wales grew wider. New counties were created in Wales, and a new system of law was introduced. A Council of Wales and the Marches (as the borders were called) set up by Henry VII had not been very effective. Henry VIII gave the Council new powers, strengthened by the county organization.

Wales' own system of lawcourts was extended into the new counties. Each county now had a sheriff, responsible to the king, and justices of the peace were appointed from local landowners to administer the law. However, the new system of law and order was carried out in English, not Welsh. People who spoke only Welsh had no hope of taking part in the official life of the country.

'For Wales – see England'

From this time forward, Welsh landowners became part of the public life enjoyed by rich people in England and Wales. They helped to enforce the legal system, they sent their sons to schools and to English universities, and they became members of Parliament. They were often remote from the ordinary people of Wales who worked on the land or rented farms from them. Even if they spoke Welsh at home, the landowners spoke English in their official lives. Their tenants and workers spoke Welsh. In these ways, throughout the next two centuries, the pattern of life that divides Wales was established. The colonization of Wales, begun by invasion, had reached into Welsh society itself.

The eighteenth and nineteenth centuries in Wales brought important changes. New industries growing up in the iron works and coal mines of the South Wales valleys changed both the countryside and people's lives. People began to leave rural Wales in the hope of finding a better life with more money in the south. They did not often find what they had hoped for. In 1831, because of low wages and the high price of bread, conditions became so bad, that there was an armed uprising in Merthyr Tydfil.

In North Wales the new industries were copper mining in Anglesey and slate quarrying in Snowdonia. The quarry workers at the Penrhyn quarry went on strike several times for better pay

Life in the Welsh mining villages during the nineteenth century was very hard. Men, women and children over five all worked down the pits for very poor wages. They rarely saw daylight as they worked long shifts. This newspaper illustration of 1873 shows pit-girls during a strike that attempted to improve wages and conditions.

and working arrangements. One of their strikes, from 1901 to 1903, was the longest in British industrial history. All these new industries, in both North and South Wales, were privately owned. The iron and coal owners in the south, and the quarry owners in the north, became rich at the expense of the thousands of labourers who worked for them. Some of the owners had Welsh connections, but they were mostly English business people. The pattern of land ownership changed as well. Families who became rich as industry grew, bought or extended their estates. While the life and language of Wales lived on at the level of the ordinary people of the country, the owners of the wealth created by Wales, like the lawgivers, were English.

A new nationalism

In the second half of the nineteenth century a movement for Home Rule was founded. There was a growing interest and pride in being Welsh. The setting up of Welsh newspapers, and of the London-based Cymrodorion Society, helped to focus attention on the subject. In 1856, a new Welsh national anthem *Hen Wlad fy Nhadau* (Land of My Fathers) was composed. The University of Wales was established in 1872. Although it was at first a college of London University, in 1893 it gained the right to grant its own degrees. At the end of the nineteenth century, Wales had become a country where there was more and better education for its children than ever before. New industries had led to the growth of an industrial base with new towns in the south. New or improved roads and the coming of the railways had opened up the country. The people were non-conformist in religion, they were radical in politics and they had a renewed spirit of nationalism.

At the beginning of the present century Wales was prospering. There was plenty of work, and agriculture and industry seemed to be growing. During the First World War the entire country was involved in the war effort. Women worked on the land and in industry, alongside those men who were not fighting. Britain's war effort was led by its first Welsh Prime Minister, David Lloyd George.

However, when the war ended in 1918, the next years brought depression to Wales. Coal and steel were not in such high demand and these industries declined. Pits closed and there was massive unemployment. Out of a total working population of 1.25 million, a quarter of a million were unemployed, and a further quarter of a million emigrated to other countries.

Changing politics

The number of Welsh speakers began to fall, and the influence of religion in Wales declined. In politics, the Liberal Party lost much support in Wales, as people began to turn to the Labour Party. Since the 1930s, Welsh Labour MPs have often led the Labour Party. There has been another Welsh Prime Minister, James Callaghan, and there have also been Welsh Leaders of the Opposition such as Michael Foot and Neil Kinnock. It was a Welshman, Aneurin (Nye) Bevan, who set up the National Health Service during the 1940s. By 1966, the Labour Party had won the support of people in 32 of the 36 Welsh constituencies. Wales was given its own Secretary of State in 1964.

This century has also seen a rise in support for the Welsh national party, Plaid Cymru, which was founded in 1925. The first Plaid seat at Westminster was won by Gwynfor Evans for Carmarthen in the 1960s, and there are now three Plaid MPs. A new campaign for stronger Welsh

During the 1930s, there was a great deal of unemployment in Wales. The government tried to retrain and educate the workers in the traditional coal mining and steel industries, so that they would be able to find work in other areas. This schoolroom at Merthyr Tydfil was run by the Ministry of Labour.

control of Welsh affairs has been launched in Wales, and it involves members of different political parties.

Political parties

The chief British political parties (Labour, Conservative, Liberal and Social Democrat) are all active in Wales, together with Plaid Cymru. The nationalists would like Wales to be independent and to become a separate political nation from England. Some members of the other parties support increased self-government for Wales, known as devolution. There is a campaign for a Welsh Assembly, which supports devolution and

After the slumps and World War during the 1930s and 1940s, there were empty or derelict cottages all over Wales. Many of these were bought very cheaply by people in England for holiday homes. This has caused much resentment among the local people and occasionally a weekend cottage is burnt in protest.

consists of members of all political parties. The campaign would like to see government based in Wales rather than in London and with greater responsibilities than the present Welsh Office.

Some political groups have adopted violent tactics in their attempt to make Wales independent. They have set fire not only to the homes of English people in Wales, but also to the offices of estate agents who advertise Welsh homes for sale in England.

The sense of Wales as a separate nation, both politically and culturally, is strong amongst some parts of Welsh society. The wish for more independent government reflects this feeling.

Government today

Welsh voters elect 38 members of Parliament to the House of Commons in London. These MPs take part in the government of the United Kingdom (England, Wales, Scotland and Northern Ireland) and they also have a special responsibility to their own voters in Wales. Welsh affairs are discussed in Parliament in the Welsh Grand Committee. In each sitting, or session, of Parliament time is given to discussing the business of Wales as a whole.

The Secretary of State for Wales has a seat in the highest group of government ministers, the British Cabinet. The Secretary of State also has a separate department, the Welsh Office. This is

The Welsh Office in Wales' capital city, Cardiff, houses the civil servants who advise the Secretary of State for Wales.

Dr Dafydd Elis Thomas addresses the Welsh national party's annual conference. Although the members of Parliament for Wales sit in Parliament in England, a sense of nationalism encouraged the Welsh to have their own political party, called Plaid Cymru.

directly responsible for some areas of government in Wales and has a staff of civil servants to advise the Secretary of State. Among advisory bodies which work closely with the Welsh Office are the Welsh Development Agency and the Welsh Health Promotion Authority. The Secretary's job is to keep the government informed about Welsh matters and to make sure that the interests of the people of Wales are not forgotten in wider government concerns.

Since 1978, Wales has elected four members to the European Parliament in Strasbourg to represent North Wales, Mid- and West Wales, South-East Wales and South Wales.

Government responsibilities

Local government in Wales is on two levels: county and district. There are eight counties – Gwynedd, Clwyd, Powys, Dyfed, Mid-Glamorgan, South Glamorgan, West Glamorgan and Gwent. They are responsible for social services, transport, education, the police, fire services and planning. The 37 districts in Wales are responsible for local services.

In many parts of the country there are also Community Councils, elected by the people of a village or part of a town. Such councils look after the interests of small areas and advise District Councils on the needs of local people. Community councillors are voluntary, they are not paid for their work.

4 Religion

Religion has played an important part in Welsh people's lives. It has shaped their thinking and become part of the fabric of Welsh society. Today, religion is still very much a part of everyday life for many people, though not as much as in the past.

Christianity is the religion of most people of Wales and has been for many centuries. Some of the earliest churches are more than 1300 years old, and can still be seen in remote parts of Wales.

However, there are also other religions in Wales today. The larger towns and cities have Jewish, Muslim, Sikh and Hindu communities. Religion does not prevent people from taking part in the life of the wider community as once it did in Wales. Two hundred years ago, no one who was not a Christian, and also a member of the Anglican Church, could hold any position in the community. Even 100 years ago a member of a non-Christian religion would have found it hard to be accepted. Recently a Muslim religious leader, or *imam*, has served as a chaplain to the South Glamorgan County Council.

Religion in the past

Everywhere in Wales there are signs of religion in past ages, even of an earlier religion than Christianity. Burial chambers and lonely standing stones are reminders that more than 2000 years ago there were people in Wales who had their own faiths and beliefs. There was, for example, a religion involving a priest-teacher group called the Druids. Anglesey was an important Druid centre.

Early Christianity

The Celtic Christian Church began to grow in Wales from about 1400 years ago. Christianity came to Wales from the east as part of the Roman invasion of Britain, and also from the west, from the Celts of Ireland. The Celtic saints, or travelling preachers, set up small churches wherever they went. These were the first *illans* or parishes. All over Wales there are place-names which begin with *Llan,* such as Llandudno, Llanddewi, Llantrisant. The longest place-name in Wales has

Tiny chapels were built by Celtic Christians all over Wales. St Govan's chapel was built by the early Christians on the cliffs of the Pembrokeshire coast. It is said that there are more steps that lead to the chapel than away from it.

the name of two saints in it: Llanfairpwllgwyngyllgogerychwyrndrobwllllantysiliogogogoch! It means: *St Mary's Church by the pool of the white hazel trees, near the rapid whirlpool, by the red cave of the Church of St Tysilio.*

As well as the few tiny early churches that remain, and the many place-names, there are other signs of Christianity in Wales through the centuries. The Celtic crosses of the early church, and the ruins of the abbeys and monasteries of the eleventh to fourteenth centuries are both reminders of the continuing Christian tradition. At one time, the monasteries owned huge areas of land in Wales. This land was sold or given away by King Henry VIII when he disbanded the

St David's cathedral was built in south-west Wales during the twelfth century. It was a pilgrimage centre for the shrine of St David, who is the patron saint of Wales. The cathedral is surrounded by a city that is little more than a village, and is the smallest cathedral city in Britain.

monasteries in 1536 and 1539. The head of the Church at that time was the Pope in Rome. Henry VIII saw that as a threat to his own power and declared himself to be head of the Church. Since that time the king or queen of England has also been head of the state Church known as the Anglican Church or Church of England.

By the end of the 1600s, people were no longer in danger of losing their lives if they did not belong to the state Church, as they had been for the previous 150 years. The Anglican Church had become the established Church of the country. Yet many people thought that the Church was out of touch with the needs of ordinary people. It had become the Church of rich landowners, the lawyers and the judges.

About 20 per cent of the adult population are members of a Christian Church, and all denominations except the Roman Catholic Church report a decline in membership over the last five years. However, there are signs that this decline is slowing down.

The Dissenters

People who did not agree with the state Church were called Dissenters. In the 1730s, one Dissenter, Griffith Jones of Llanddowror in Dyfed, set up a system of schools in Wales. It brought education to more than 200 000 people at a time when most people could neither read nor write.

The textbook in these schools was the Bible, which had been first translated into Welsh in 1588. A new Welsh translation was published in 1988 to mark the 400th anniversary of this event.

Most people in Wales spoke Welsh. The language of the lawcourts and the language of the upper classes had been English, ever since the union between England and Wales in 1536. However, the language of the working people was Welsh. Being taught to read and write in their own language was very important for ordinary people. Although the preachers and teachers of the new movement wanted people to be educated so that they could read the Bible for themselves, learning to read and write opened up a whole new world for the Welsh. They began to think for themselves in a new way.

The Methodists

From this early beginning, the history of independent thought and action by the working people of Wales can be traced. When John Wesley and other preachers came to Wales they found that a great many people were ready to listen. In 1811, the Methodist Church in Wales was formed and quickly spread throughout the country. The first Dissenting preachers had often preached in the open air, in country districts far from churches. Now people began to get together to raise money to build their own places of worship. These buildings were called chapels to show that they were different from the Anglican churches. The chapels of the people who did not wish to belong, or conform, to the Anglican Church were soon seen all over Wales. As well as Methodists, there were Baptists, Quakers, Congregationalists and Presbyterians. They were all different from the Anglicans, with their own beliefs and ways of worship. They were, and still are, called

Religion in Wales

Membership of Christian Churches (1985)

	Members	Buildings
Anglican	115 896	1521
Methodist	22 561	415
Baptist	45 611	785
Presbyterian	84 750	1212
Other	84 248	1144
Roman Catholic	146 673	324
Orthodox	1 136	6
Other religions		
Jewish	837	2
Buddhist	2 000	10
Hindu	5 000	1
Islam	14 000	5
Sikh	25 000	20
Others	10 000	10

During the eighteenth and nineteenth centuries there was a great revival of interest in religion in Wales. Several breakaway Protestant, or non-conformist sects became so popular that services often had to be taken outside, as the crowd was too large for the chapel.

non-conformists. Their preaching, their teaching and their services were all in the Welsh language.

Chapel life

These newer groups or denominations gave working people in Wales a new sense of purpose. People became involved in the organization of their chapel, and the chapels became centres for social life as well as Sunday services. In towns and villages today the simple buildings of the non-conformists are very much part of the landscape.

Thomas Charles, one of the preachers who led the Methodists out of the Anglican Church, also started the Sunday Schools movement. These schools formed the basis for education in Wales for most of the nineteenth century. They were held in the chapels every Sunday, and the children were taught to read and write.

By the 1850s, the Anglican Church was no longer the main Church of Wales. A survey in 1851 showed that almost 80 per cent of Welsh people were members of non-conformist churches. Many people thought that the Anglican Church should no longer be the official state Church in Wales, and they began to press for change. In 1920, the Anglican Church in Wales separated from the state and is no longer the established Church. Its bishops, unlike the English bishops, do not sit in the House of Lords in Parliament.

The history of religion in Wales over the past 300 years has also been the history of the growth of new ideas. The chapels were places where people gathered on Sundays for services, and during the

For 200 years the influence of the chapel controlled how people lived or thought. In many villages there were several chapels, often side by side, and even today many are well attended.

week for other meetings, such as prayer-meetings and Bible study. It was there, too, that adults as well as children were taught to read and write. Cultural life also centred on the chapel. Music, especially singing, is part of Welsh life, and the chapels were great holders of musical festivals and competitions, called *eisteddfodau*. Singing festivals are part of the national life of Wales today.

New thinking

People who belonged to the non-conforming chapels were often the same people who helped to bring new ideas to politics in Wales. A different kind of community life gradually grew up. The study groups at chapel led to all kinds of new thinking in politics as well as religion. The women and men who helped to run their chapels gained experience in talking and exchanging ideas on all sorts of subjects. Religion may have given them the new ideas about justice and equality, but politics was for many people the way to make those ideas become real. They began to ask questions about why they could not vote for their members of Parliament, or why many people did not earn enough money to live on. Then they began to try to make life better for working people. Members of Welsh chapels up and down the land joined the new political parties. Amongst the strongest supporters of these Liberal and Labour parties over the past century have been Welsh chapel people. Taking part in the life of the chapel came to mean that Welsh working people became more involved in the life of the country itself.

This pattern can be seen today. At the last General Election, as in many in the last 50 years, almost the whole of the South Wales area voted Labour. Many organizations such as the Youth Movement, *Urdd*, or the womens organization, *Merched y wawr*, developed out of or are linked with chapel activities. They are important in the life of Wales today and are part of what gives Wales its special identity. In education, politics and the cultural life of Wales, religion has played its part in forming the character of the country.

5 Getting around

Roads, railways, ports and airports connect Wales with other countries. During the past 20 years communications inside Wales have improved a great deal, but it is still easier to travel in and out of the country than it is to go from north to south inside Wales itself. Caernarfon and Carmarthen seem further apart than Holyhead and London and there is still no direct road or rail link between North and South Wales.

The high mountains and wide rivers of Wales are no longer the barriers they were once. In 1966, the long awaited road bridge across the Severn River opened, and it is possible to drive from the south-east of England into south-west Wales in

The Severn bridge spans the river near its estuary. The bridge was built in the 1960s and is 988 metres (3240 feet long). It connects England and South Wales, and carries a great deal of traffic – both goods vehicles and tourists.

about four hours. South Wales' main airport at Cardiff is an international one. There is a smaller airport at Swansea that handles charter and business flights. The north is not so well served for air travel. Its nearest airports are at Manchester and Birmingham, several hours journey away.

Going by rail

Rail services connect the main Welsh cities with London and with one another, and there are link services with the smaller towns. The main line into Mid-Wales runs to Aberystwyth from Shrewsbury. There are connections to the north along the western coast, which is one of the most spectacular routes in the country.

Wales is unusual in Britain in still having very small stations, such as this isolated one at Tygwyn near Harlech. During the 1960s, most small railway lines in Britain were closed as an economy measure, and only a few in isolated areas survive.

In the north, the line from Chester to Holyhead also runs along the coast, with links to Betws-y-coed, and to the slate town of Blaenau Ffestiniog. These towns are now popular with summer visitors, as is Llandudno.

Two famous suspension bridges, designed by Thomas Telford more than 100 years ago, can be seen by passengers travelling by rail along the coast. The line runs alongside the old suspension bridge over the Conwy estuary, and skirts Conwy Castle. After leaving Bangor the train crosses the Menai Strait to Anglesey. The line goes over another engineering marvel, the Britannia Bridge, a tubular bridge designed by Robert Stephenson in the nineteenth century. From this bridge Telford's Menai suspension bridge can be seen. The North Wales line continues across Anglesey to the port of Holyhead and the ferry service to Ireland.

Going by sea

Sea links to and from Wales are hundreds of years old. Wales has more than 1200 kilometres (750 miles) of coastline, and several main ports. People travelling into Wales from Ireland cross from Dun Laoghaire to Holyhead, from Cork to Swansea or from Rosslare to Fishguard. From each of these ports there are good road and rail links.

Other ports deal with goods rather than passengers. Although Holyhead is the only deep-water container port in North Wales, South Wales is well served by the five ports of Swansea, Port Talbot, Cardiff, Barry and Newport, from which goods such as iron ore, coal or food products enter and leave Wales.

The snow-covered mountains of North Wales rise behind the Menai Bridge. When he built the suspension bridge over the Menai Straits in 1825, Thomas Telford greatly improved the route from London to Holyhead, the main ferry port for Ireland. Later a separate box tunnel bridge was built to carry the railway from Wales to Anglesey.

In the past

In the last 60 years the roads in Wales have improved out of all recognition. Before that time there were no motorways, and those roads that did exist were far below the standard of even second class roads of today.

The story of roads in Wales began when the Romans reached Wales nearly 2000 years ago. Straight, wide roads with strong foundations were built to carry soldiers and goods from the Romans' forts into Wales. The remains of some of these roads can still be seen today.

After the Romans left there was little or no road building in Wales for several centuries. Then about 300 years ago the first Turnpike Trusts were set up to raise money to improve the roads. Travellers had to pay a toll each time they used a road. The money was collected at tollgate houses built all along the roads. However, paying tolls to use a road could make a journey to market for example very expensive, and people disliked them. In some places in South Wales tollgates were even destroyed in riots. It was not until county councils and central government began to spend money on roads that any improvement was seen.

During the nineteenth century, several canals were built to transport slate and other heavy goods. The Llangollen canal in Clwyd carried barges across some steep valleys on superb feats of engineering, such as the Pontcysyllte aqueduct. The canal now provides an important tourist attraction.

Most of the network of road, rail and water communications that now exists in Wales in fact came into being in the last 200 years. Up till then, travel to, from and within Wales was difficult. Invaders nearly all came by sea or river and the Romans built a port at Caerleon in Gwent.

Canals

The iron and coal industries in South Wales and the slate industry in the north needed better transport systems to carry their goods away for sale. For a long time, it was easier to move goods by water than by land. Sometimes rivers were not the answer because they were not deep enough, or they flowed in the wrong direction. For this reason canals were built in many places.

The canals were linked to the workplaces by an early form of railway in which horses pulled carts along wooden or iron rails. On one of these early trackways Richard Trevithick tried out what was probably the first steam engine. It pulled 10 tons of iron and carried 70 people along the tramway between Penydarren ironworks and the Glamorgan canal in South Wales.

Railways developed quickly, and by the 1830s, tracks were being built to connect workplaces to ports. The railways carried people as well as goods to the ports. Before the London to Holyhead rail link was built, the stage coach took more than 28 hours to travel the 435 kilometres (250 miles) journey. The growth of railways meant that Wales could now be visited by people who simply wanted to see what the country was like. It was the start of a new industry, tourism, which was to become very important to Wales.

6 Living off the land

Wales is mostly a land of small farms. Outside the business centres of the south, which grew up with the coal and steel industries of the last 150 years, agriculture and tourism are the main ways of making a living.

Without some knowledge of how the land used to be owned and farmed, and where people used to live, it is difficult to understand some of the changes that have taken place over the last 150 years.

Where people lived

At the beginning of the nineteenth century, about 80 per cent of the population lived in rural Wales. The pattern of life had changed little from 1188 when a monk, Gerald of Wales, rode around the country and wrote about how the Welsh lived in scattered homesteads, tending animals and living on a diet of meat, oatmeal, milk, butter and cheese. They used their land to graze animals and grow a few basic cereal crops. In Gerald's time the population was about a quarter of a million, and over the 700 years to 1800 it had only increased to half a million. Since that time the population has grown to its present 2.8 million in less than 200 years.

Nearly all Welsh people in the nineteenth century gained their living from the land. They either worked on it as farmers or farm labourers, or they were craft workers who supplied the farms with household goods or tools for farm work. There was some industrial work in the south in small coal and iron works, in the north-east there were charcoal furnaces, and in Anglesey there were copper mines. Changes in farming methods came slowly. Wealthy landowners were introducing change into English farming but their ideas took at least 50 years to spread into Wales.

Welsh people in general lived on farms or in small villages. The few towns were either market centres such as Carmarthen or Caernarfon, or ports such as Swansea or Conwy.

The landowners

Most of the land in Wales at that time was owned by about 100 great landowning families, each family controlling more than 2000 hectares (5000 acres). These families were powerful and influential in the life of Wales. They rented out farms to tenant farmers, with whom they rarely had any contact.

About 1000 owners farmed land of between 200 and 2000 hectares (500 and 5000 acres), and they also rented out farmland. All farmers relied on their farm produce for food, but tenants also had to pay their rents in cash, which they found difficult. The poorest farmers found it hard to make any kind of living. Agricultural progress of any kind was slow, because of the isolation of country areas through lack of roads.

The growth of industry in Wales from the beginning of the nineteenth century up to about 1914 changed the old pattern of life for ever. The increased use of machinery on farms meant fewer jobs. There was also the possibility of better wages in other jobs, so that many people left the countryside to look for work in the new industrial

This small farm near Aberystwyth is typical of Mid-Wales with its mixture of sheep and small amounts of cereal crops.

towns. Improved and new roads, canals and railways brought contact with a wider world and still more changes.

Change in ownership

Better transport meant that farm produce could reach new markets. Milk could be transported over greater distances, and Welsh milk was sold as far away as London. The expansion of shipping and the invention of refrigeration meant Welsh produce found markets all over the world, as it does today.

One of the biggest changes was in the ownership of the land. People who made money in industry began to buy land. By the end of the nineteenth century the number of great landowners in Wales had increased to around 600, but still, for example, only six families controlled most of Caernarfonshire. These huge estates have gradually been broken up and sold off during the last 50 years, as a result of changes in government policy on both taxation and on farming methods.

During the wars

Agriculture in Wales was affected by the two World Wars in this century. A Ministry of Food was set up in 1916, and again in 1939, to advise on food production during the wars. After the Second World War, the Ministry remained as a permanent government department. It is now called the Ministry of Agriculture, Fisheries and Food (MAFF), and it encourages farmers to produce food according to what is needed at any one time. By grants of money or tax relief, it helps farmers to plan their work and to decide what to grow.

In some ways agriculture in Wales may be

The drovers

Modern farmers take their animals to market in specially built trucks, but sheep and cattle used to be herded on foot to markets on the borders of Wales or in England. Drovers walked or rode beside the sheep and cattle for hundreds of kilometres, with only their dogs to help them. In some places the old drove roads can still be clearly seen.

Droving was a difficult and dangerous occupation, especially when carrying money from the sale of the animals back to the farms. During the nineteenth century, special banks were set up so that the drovers could put their earnings into a safe place.

Sheep from the hill farms are brought into market at Llanrwst. Sheep markets like this one are held regularly in many market towns.

showing signs of coming full circle. Instead of larger and larger farms, or big estates, many young people are now farming smallholdings, perhaps as well as having another job. The use of the land is changing, as it always has, in response to the needs of the people.

Today, about three-quarters of the land is in agricultural use. The highland areas are not suitable for crop growing, and farms there raise cattle and sheep. The Welsh hillsides are dotted with hardy sheep, bred to withstand the cold

Sheep will roam over a large area of moorland. It takes a long time to round them up, but today's shepherds use motorbikes or four-wheel drive vehicles to reach the remoter parts of their farms.

winds, rain and snow of the uplands.

Sheep stealing is an ever-present threat to farmers. Today's rustlers do not come on horseback with guns and ropes as they did in the Wild West of the USA. They come in fast trucks, often at night. The Welsh police have many cases of animal stealing reported to them each year.

Dairy farming

In lowland areas, where the climate is milder and the soils more fertile, there are dairy farms and crops are grown on arable farms. Anglesey in the north and Gwent and West Dyfed in the south are important areas for farms of these kinds. Barley, oats, potatoes and other vegetables are grown, as well as cereal crops. Most of the mixed corn crop is used for feeding livestock.

In recent years, since Britain joined the European Community (EC), milk quotas have been introduced. This means that there is a limit on the amount of milk a farm may produce. Since many farmers had built up large herds of dairy cattle, the milk quotas brought problems. However, farmers have now begun to find new ways of using milk. As well as the traditional butter, cream and cheese, yogurt and skimmed milk are now being produced. Cheese has been made on Welsh farms for local use for hundreds of years, but nearly all of it was sold at market. Wales is again becoming known for its good quality farm-produced cheeses, from the ever popular Caerphilly to newer kinds such as Pencarreg.

Other changes are happening to farming in Wales, in the same way as there are changes in farming patterns right across the European Community. Farmers have to find different ways of using their land. During the last 80 years many farmers gave up the old ways of mixed farming and have been growing only cereals, or perhaps raising only cattle, for instance. Now that the market for their produce has grown smaller, they have had to look for other ways of making a living. Some farmers have gone into the tourist business. They offer farm holidays, with pony-trekking or fishing as an added attraction.

Organic farming

Some farmers have changed their methods of farming and are now producing food which has been grown naturally, or organically. This means that no chemical fertilizers or pesticides have been used, either on the land or on the crop itself. It takes several years to change over to fully organic farming, but more and more farmers are doing so. There are now more than 1000 farms in the United Kingdom registered as organic farms. The demand for food produced in this way is growing. People think it is healthier, and that organic farming does not harm the land itself. Many of the artificial fertilizers and pesticides used on farms in the last half century have been shown to have harmful effects on both the land and wildlife.

The Centre for Alternative Technology was set up at Machynlleth to encourage people to explore new ways of farming and using energy. This display shows how food waste can be simply recycled into fertilizer.

When the tide goes out on the estuary at Penclawdd in South Wales, wide expanses of sand and mud are exposed. These are traditional cockle beds and cockle gatherers are still seen filling their baskets at low tide.

Fishing

Fishing has always been a way of making a living for people living around the coasts of Wales, but the large fishing fleets of the last hundred years are now only a memory. A recent development in Wales is fish farming. Salmon, trout, cockles, mussels, lobsters and oysters are raised on fish farms and are finding a market in shops all over Britain and abroad. One special kind of sea trout, the sewin, is found only in Wales.

Inland, people fished from small boats called coracles, so light that they could be carried home. Out along the cocklebeds of the southern shores it was once common to see people gathering cockles.

They had donkeys to carry them, or simply carried the cockles themselves in great baskets strapped to their backs. Both cocklegathering and coracle fishing can still be seen but very rarely now.

Seaweed or kelp was once gathered from the seashore and made into a paste that could be fried and eaten. This delicacy, called laverbread, is still made in some areas of the south. Seaweed is today used as a fertilizer for the land and as part of special diets, usually in tablet form.

Forestry

Most of the old Welsh oak, ash and beech woods have gone, although they are now being preserved in areas where this kind of forest remains. The great sweeps of dark green which cover many Welsh hillsides are forests planted and managed by the Forestry Commission. More than a quarter of the Forestry Commission's timber production in the United Kingdom comes from Wales.

In recent years, people have begun to think again about the kinds of trees that should be planted for timber. Those that have been planted up to now do not provide habitats for the animals and birds that once lived in the forests. In addition, when they are felled, the land where they grew is sour and spoiled. Now people are more aware of this damage to the environment and new ways of managing the forests are being considered.

7 Old and new industries

At one time, to think of Wales was to think of heavy industry. 'Coal was king' and coal made Wales known throughout the world. The valleys of South Wales, with their pithead wheels and their rows of tiny terraced houses, were most people's picture of working Wales. The coal, iron and steel of South Wales built and provided fuel for the railways, factories and machinery of the western world and slates from the quarries of North Wales roofed houses all over the world.

Taft Merthyr Colliery in Mid-Glamorgan is 638 metres (2093 feet) deep. It was first mined in 1924. In the 1930s the mine produced about 600 000 tonnes of coal a year and employed 1600 men. Today, it produces 650 000 tonnes with only about 600 men.

Today, the heavy industries which for 200 years provided work for Wales are in decline. At the beginning of this century, there were 240 pits in the South Wales coalfields. Now there are only nine, and some of those are under threat of closure. Thousands of miners have lost their jobs, and communities that were built on coal no longer have the pit as the centre of their working lives.

It is a similar story in the steel towns of South Wales. Now only the very large steel works such as Llanwern are providing work. In other areas where steel was the main source of work, such as Shotton in North Wales, steelworks have closed and thousands of people have lost their way of making a living.

Port Talbot is important for shipping heavy goods in and out of Wales. The port has been enlarged to accommodate bulk carriers of oil and iron ore. Large oil refineries dominate the skyline.

New technology

In the same way that Wales was at the heart of industrial change when the mines and ironworks meant jobs for everyone, so it is now. New technology has once more brought new jobs to the country.

Welsh coal still provides eight per cent of Britain's deep-mined and 11 per cent of its open-cast coal production, but all kinds of new industries have come to Wales. Ports such as Milford Haven and Port Talbot in South Wales handle timber and wood products, fruit, grain, foodstuffs, chemicals and manufactured goods. They also ship iron ore, steel and tinplate as well as other metals such as lead, zinc and aluminium.

New businesses

The British government is encouraging people to find work in new industries, and to set up their own businessess. The Welsh Development Agency gives grants to new small businesses and advises people on how to start up on their own. A government department called Winvest is responsible for attracting new businesses to Wales and it has been very successful. Today, one in five of all jobs in Welsh manufacturing industries are the result of Winvest's work.

As well as large companies which come into Wales from outside, new, smaller companies are starting up throughout Wales. Some of these companies have become multi-national businesses. The Laura Ashley fabrics and clothing empire, for example, started in a small town in Mid-Wales, and is now known all over the world. Other businesses remain small, but are still very successful at what they produce, whether it is garden furniture, model cottages or designs for tapestries and cushions.

Newer industries in Wales include computer parts and products, optics, electro-acoustics, office furniture, automotive and electrical engineering, oil refining and electricity generating.

Water and electricity

In the last 50 years the need for electricity has risen steadily, and new ways have had to be found of providing it cheaply. One of Wales' richest natural resources is water, and this is being used to make electricity. There are several hydro-electricity schemes in Wales. The newest scheme, which is also the biggest in Europe, is at Dinorwig in the mountains of Snowdonia. Most of the Dinorwig scheme is hidden inside the mountains.

Half of Wales' water is exported. The lakes and reservoirs of North and Mid-Wales supply water to many large towns and cities of England, such as Birmingham and Manchester. About five per cent of the workers in Wales are employed in the water and energy industries.

The Welsh Water Authority manages the water services in Wales. The Authority is responsible for the distribution of water and for making sure that it is clean. Rivers, freshwater fisheries, sewage treatment, disposal and drainage are all the responsibility of the WWA. Some Welsh reservoirs are used as recreation areas, and the WWA also looks after these. Some of these jobs are to be taken over by a new Rivers Authority, and some will soon be privatized. This means that

Wales has plenty of rainfall so large dams such as the Craig Goch Dam in the Elan Valley, Powys have been built. The reservoirs they create supply water to large industrial cities in England.

they will be sold by the government, and will be run by private companies.

Nuclear power is another source of energy. There are at present two nuclear power stations in Wales, one at Wylfa on the Anglesey coast, and one at Trawsfynydd, also in North Wales.

The challenge of change

Unemployment is high in Wales. More than 14 per cent of the people are out of work. In some areas where everyone worked in the same industry, such as coal or steel, the closure of local works has meant that whole communities lost their jobs. In spite of these setbacks, people all over the country are meeting this challenge of change in their working lives. More and more people are either working for themselves or in small companies instead of being employed in one of the giant industries as in the past.

Most people in Wales now work in service industries. Offices, shops, hotels and restaurants, building, education, health and social services, provide jobs for nearly 70 per cent of the working population in Wales.

Some of the areas that suffered badly when the traditional industries declined, have been made into special development areas. This means that any new industries that are started in these areas will be given financial help either by the government or the local council. They may not have to pay very much for their factories, for example, or the rates they pay to the council may be low. This kind of encouragement has helped to provide new jobs.

Moving to the jobs

Since people usually live near their place of work, the way industry has grown over the last 200 years has also dictated where Welsh people live. About 70 per cent of the population is shared between South Wales and the north-east, in and around the towns that grew up when the coal mines and steel works were opened. Then, as other industries have come to the south, people have left the rural areas in search of new jobs. Mid-Wales in particular has become depopulated for this reason. The most serious result is that its young people have had to leave. Many organizations as well as the government are trying to attract young people and new industries back into Mid-Wales. The Development Board for Rural Wales was formed

The Welsh are trying to create new industry and restore their countryside. They have reclaimed large areas of land that were ruined by mining waste. This complex of units for small industries and crafts has been built on reclaimed land.

to encourage growth in the area. It provides factories, housing and advice to small businesses which employ under 200 people. It also has a special responsibility for a new town in Powys called Newtown.

Now that industry in Wales is changing so dramatically, Welsh independence is coming to the fore. The determination that led Welsh workers to strike for better work conditions or to protest against injustice and low pay still exists. Small enterprises are springing up all over Wales. One young man has set up a new textile business in Penmaenmawr. A group of women in West Wales have formed a co-operative making shoes. An

Anglesey family has opened a butterfly farm. A Gwent family keeps bees. Each of these small businesses is built on hope and help, but they are all providing a living for their workers.

Tourism
Gerald of Wales, the monk who travelled through Wales around 800 years ago, was probably the first tourist to visit the country and to write about it. Ever since his time people have been coming to Wales and have appreciated its beauty and its way of life.

Action holidays
About nine million tourists visit the country each year, and the tourist industry is now an important source of income for many Welsh people. In rural areas, tourism is the second most important industry after agriculture. In holiday towns around the coast tourism is the main source of income for many people.

Some visitors come to Wales for the beauty of the scenery and the peacefulness of life. They walk in the hills or sail around the coasts. They fish or simply do nothing! Other people want a more energetic holiday, and for them there are all kinds of outdoor activities, from climbing, canoeing and ponytrekking to visiting castles or other places of interest. Climbers of world class, such as Chris Bonnington have trained for their Everest attempts in the mountains of Snowdonia.

Looking at the past
Visitors are often interested in the history of Wales. There are the castles of the Welsh princes

There are several climbing schools in Wales which are able to use the varied terrain to provide training in climbing all types of rock. This steep rock face near Capel Curig in Gwynedd challenges these young mountaineers.

and of the English invaders. Great houses once owned by rich people, and the cottages of ordinary people, are now open to the public. There are the forts and settlements of the Romans of 2000 years ago and the hill villages of even earlier peoples. Ruined abbeys and monasteries of the Christians, and the burial chambers and standing stones of the people who followed an older religion, can still be seen. Six thousand years of Welsh history are all around to be explored. An organization called Welsh Historic Monuments (CADW) protects and preserves about 130 of these places throughout Wales.

Museums and art galleries display some of the arts and crafts of today, for people are becoming interested in the old skills of spinning and weaving, making textiles, carving on wood and slate, and producing pottery.

Rural or folk museums in many parts of Wales show how country people lived and worked. Farm tools or farmhouse furniture give tourists some idea of what life was like for ordinary Welsh women and men in the past.

The Museum of Welsh Folk Life at St Fagans near Cardiff shows Welsh life throughout the centuries. There are even whole buildings preserved from the past. It was the first museum of its kind in Britain, and almost half a million people visit it every year.

There are also museums of industrial life. In North Wales some of the disused slate quarries have been opened to the public, showing how the quarriers worked and how the slate was cut. Small railways, such as the Tal-y-llyn or Ffestiniog lines, which used to carry the slate to the ports to be shipped overseas now carry tourists through some of Wales' most beautiful countryside.

Protecting wildlife

Changes in farming methods and the building of new roads and towns, mean that some animals and birds have lost their food and their homes. Special areas in Wales, called reserves, have been set aside

A rack railway climbs Wales's highest mountain. The small steam locomotive carries many tourists up to Snowdon's main peak, Y Wyddfa.

as places where animals and birds will be safe. The Royal Society for the Protection of Birds and the Nature Conservancy Council, among others, work in these reserves. The wildlife of Wales needs to be protected or it will die out and become extinct.

Plant life, too, is protected in parts of Wales, since some plants are now very rare because of changes in land use.

Areas of natural beauty are also being preserved, in the three national parks of Snowdonia, the Brecon Beacons and Pembroke. The National Trust in Wales owns and manages coastline, woodlands and other areas, as well as looking after many of the houses that are open to the public.

Hard work goes into preserving the beauty and

wildlife of Wales, bringing added attractions for visitors, whose numbers increase year by year.

'Keeping a welcome'

As well as income, tourism has brought special problems to parts of Wales. Tourism creates jobs and provides a living for many people, but the changes it brings may mean that the old ways of life simply disappear for ever and the Welsh language declines. Another problem is that of holiday homes. Welsh cottages have been bought as second homes that are empty for most of the year because their owners live and work elsewhere. This both destroys community life and can make it difficult for young people to find homes in local areas at prices they can afford. Small villages are particularly affected by this problem.

However, in most areas visitors will see signs with *Croeso* on them, meaning 'welcome'. The increasing numbers of visitors to Wales each year seems to show that people who come to Wales do indeed feel welcome.

8 Education

Since the end of the last century the education system in Wales has grown into the complete network of schools, colleges, university and institutes of higher education that exists today.

Education in Wales is free, and all children between the ages of five and 16 must attend school. The Department of Education and Science, part of the government of the United Kingdom, organizes education in England and Wales, and teachers are paid by the state. Every local authority has an Education Committee which looks after the schools in its area, appointing

Primary schools in rural areas often serve very remote farms. This primary school only has 30 pupils between the ages of five and 11.

teachers and maintaining school buildings. The Welsh Office, the government department based in Cardiff, is responsible for education in Wales.

When they are five years old children go to infant schools, going on to primary schools when they are seven. Secondary school begins at 11 years of age. Many children stay on at school until they are 17 or 18, when they may go on to higher education, college or university, or to some other form of training.

New curriculum

In 1988, a new Education Reform Act was passed, and teaching of a national curriculum started in 1989. School subjects are now either core subjects or foundation subjects. The core subjects are mathematics, science and English, and in schools where all subjects are taught in Welsh, Welsh is a core subject. The foundation subjects are history, geography, technology, music, art and physical education. In Wales, Welsh is a foundation subject in those schools that teach in English. Religious education is compulsory for all pupils.

About 90 per cent of the pupils of secondary school age attend mixed ability or comprehensive schools in Wales that are usually near where they live. Parents are now able to choose which schools they would prefer their children to attend. Parents are also able to take part in the running of schools on the governing bodies for each school. Some schools have school councils, which include senior pupils so that they can tell parents and teachers how they feel about the way their school is being run.

Schools inspectors are appointed by the

Secondary schools are usually large and have both boys and girls. This new comprehensive school in Pontypridd has 1000 pupils. Children from the countryside are brought in on special buses.

government for all the subjects taught in schools. Each local authority appoints special teachers' advisers and there are about 500 teachers' centres throughout England and Wales, providing information, and housing training courses and discussions.

Special schemes

In 1983, the government introduced a new scheme called the Technical and Vocational Education Initiative (TVEI) for pupils between 14 and 18 years old. It provides technical and vocational training which can lead to national qualifications. Another special educational scheme is the Microelectronic Education Support Unit, set up in 1986 to help local authorities with computer teaching in schools.

Several organizations, the largest of which is the Welsh Language Society, Cymdeithas yr Iaith Cymraeg, are campaigning for the increased use of Welsh in education. The nursery schools movement, Mudiad Ysgolion Meithrin, offers pre-school education in Welsh. There are also Welsh playgroups and day care groups for pre-school children that are privately run.

There are independent schools in Wales. These schools are privately owned and parents pay to send their children to them. However, the schools must be registered with and approved by the government. There are also schools run by religious bodies such as the Church of England or the Roman Catholic Church. All schools, whether of Christian, Jewish, Muslim or any other faith, must provide the required standard of education and must be approved by the government.

Education in the past

Before the nineteenth century, not many Welsh children had the chance to go to school. Three hundred years ago, most children were taught at home. Five hundred years ago, they could have gone to schools set up by monks in some of the monasteries. Grammar schools such as the Friars School in Bangor were set up about 400 years ago, and there were towns where churches or charities provided education for poor children. Such schools were few in number and not open to every child. Children of rich families were taught at home by tutors.

After the Civil War in England and Wales, in the 1650s, a number of schools were started in Wales by the Puritans. The Puritans were people who wanted a simpler form of Christian worship than the Church of England offered. They thought that it was important for people to be able to read and write in order to study the Bible for themselves. So the Puritans not only set up schools, they also published Welsh Bibles.

Another organization that raised money for education in Wales was the Welsh Trust led by Thomas Gouge. It provided books and Bibles for schools. However, when Gouge died in 1681, the movement did not carry on his work.

The Society for the Promotion of Christian Knowledge (SPCK) also attempted to provide education. It set up 96 schools in Wales to teach children reading, writing and arithmetic, but the schools were not well attended. Most people could not afford to let their children go to school when there was work for them to do at home or on the farm.

These early attempts to provide education did spread the idea that education was important. Books began to be written in Welsh, and between 1660 and 1730 about 500 were published. The work of the Dissenters in setting up travelling schools, and later the Sunday Schools movement, contributed to a growing belief that education should be provided for as many people as possible. At the beginning of the nineteenth century, Sunday Schools were the only schools which most working people were able to attend. The children of wealthy people were sent away to public schools in England, or to one of the very few grammar schools in Wales, or they were educated at home.

As the nineteenth century progressed, two societies were set up which were to prove very important to education in Wales. They were the British and Foreign Bible Society, founded in 1808, and the National Society, founded in 1811. The schools started by these societies ran on a monitor system. The teacher taught the older or more clever pupils, who in their turn taught other children. Although these schools cost only a few pence each week, even that small amount of money was too much for many Welsh families to find.

In 1833, the government gave its first grant to education, which helped the work of the societies. By the middle of the nineteenth century about 200 schools had been set up in Wales. There were also schools funded by mine or factory owners, such as the Guest family in Merthyr.

Education Acts

In 1847, a report on education in Wales was published. It caused an outcry, because it stated that Wales was lacking in education, and that Welsh people could not find better jobs because their language held them back. Welsh people called this government report, *Brad y Llyfrau Gleision*, the 'treason of the blue books'. Welsh schools had to teach more English, and Welsh became a second-class language. This caused a great deal of bad feeling between Welsh and English speaking people in Wales. Welsh children in some schools were forced to wear a piece of wood, the 'Welsh not' around their necks if they were caught speaking Welsh. They were also caned at the end of the day. The Education Act of 1870, which brought about a country-wide system of education, ignored the Welsh language entirely.

The University of Wales built its first college on the sea front at Aberystwyth. As the university grew larger these imposing buildings were erected further inland.

Then in 1880, an Act was passed making it compulsory for children to attend school until they were 13 years old. By the end of the century, all Welsh children were at last going to free school.

Further education

Wales has a wide range to offer for those pupils who go on to further education. The University of Wales has colleges at Aberystwyth, Bangor, Swansea, Cardiff and Lampeter. There is a Welsh College of Agriculture at Aberystwyth and a Polytechnic of Wales at Treforest. There is a Welsh College of Music and Drama, a Welsh Plant

Breeding Station, a Welsh College of Librarianship, and there are colleges of education. There are also colleges which train students who wish to become ministers of religion.

Student activity in Wales is lively. Many students have joined protests against cuts in educational spending, or marched in support of the use of the Welsh language in public life. Many courses in colleges can now be studied in Welsh, and many Welsh people would like to see the use of the language grow. Since the attempts to ignore Welsh in the educational system in Wales in the last century, its use has been brought back into schools and colleges as people have realized that it was in danger of dying out.

9 Welfare and housing

Health care in Wales is provided by the government through the National Health Service (NHS). All workers have to pay part of their earnings towards the National Insurance scheme, which helps to finance the health service, and provides other benefits such as sickness or unemployment pay.

The Department of Health and Social Security is a central government department. Regional authorities look after health care on a broad basis, and local health authorities on a regional or county basis.

People in Wales register with a doctor near their home. They do not pay for treatment by the doctor nor for hospital care, but they have to pay a charge for any medication they may need. Some people, such as pregnant women, or the elderly, do not pay these charges. Charges are also made for dental treatment and for spectacles but they are much less costly than private treatment would be. If Welsh people wish to pay for private health care they may do so, just as elsewhere in Britain.

Health programmes

The Welsh Health Promotion Authority was set up in 1987 to advise the government on health education. It plans and carries out health programmes to make people more aware of their own health. Campaigns such as 'Heartbeat Wales', which is trying to make people more aware of the dangers of heart disease, are part of the work of the Authority. WHPA is also involved with

The gaunt faces of these miners in the early 1900s show that they were not well fed or healthy. Many of them suffered from a disease caused by coal dust in the lungs. The National Health Service, started in 1948, introduced proper medical care for everyone and the health of the miners has improved dramatically.

drugs education in schools and colleges, and public education on health dangers such as the spread of AIDS.

Personal social services are provided at local level throughout the country. Family care and care in residential homes and home care for elderly or disabled people, or people with mental disabilities are all provided by the local authorities.

Caring in the community

As well as the state system of care, there are hundreds of voluntary organizations which help to care for people with special needs. Some of these organizations are helped by grants from the government, others exist wholly on money which they raise themselves, or which is given by the public. Some voluntary agencies such as Welsh Women's Aid, provide direct services as well as information to help make people more aware of other people's needs. Welsh Women's Aid provides refuges where women who are victims of domestic violence may find safety and help. Organizations such as Age Concern or the National Society for the Prevention of Cruelty to Children also publish information and advise the government on social policy.

The Wales Council for Voluntary Action co-ordinates the voluntary groups and publishes information to keep voluntary workers in touch with one another.

Housing

Every Welsh region has a mixture of housing, from the isolated country farm to the busy local town, where there will be both fine but costly dwellings and smaller, and cheaper houses and flats.

In larger towns there is both public and private housing. Public, or council, housing is provided by the local council for people to rent at a reasonable or fair price. It was originally intended for people who could not afford to buy their own houses. Today, council tenants have the right to buy their homes or flats from the council.

Isolated farms, such as this one, dot the hills and mountains of Wales. During the winter snows they are often completely cut off.

Since 1989, council tenants also have the right to choose their landlords. They may, if they wish, decide that a private company would give them better service than the local council. So if a private company or housing association wishes to buy and run a housing estate, the tenants may agree to this form of management.

Private housing provides a variety of homes in many price ranges. The cost of housing varies depending on the popularity of an area, the size and style of the building. Many people have to live near their work, and some people are too poor to have any choice about where they live. They cannot afford to move even if they wish to. Organizations such as Shelter try to help homeless people, or people with housing difficulties, and they try to make governments more aware of the problems.

In some towns in Wales local companies provided housing for their workers. Much of this industrial housing was built quickly and cheaply as the quarries or mines grew. Such housing now has its own character, and is recognizable as a 'coal town' or 'slate village'. The hillside terraces of the South Wales valleys are world-famous. In many areas this type of workers' housing has been pulled

Terraces of cottages built by the quarry or mine owners are to be found throughout Wales. These houses at Blaenau Ffestiniog are overshadowed by mountains of waste from the slate quarry.

down to make way for new housing, but in some places the houses have been modernized. The solid stone and slate of the quarry cottages can still be seen all over North Wales.

In country areas the coming of industry in the 1800s led to the building of some special types of houses. Roads were improved, canals and railways were built, and houses for their workers were built also. Farm workers, if they did not live in outbuildings or sleep in barns, often built small cabins on common land. There was also a custom which allowed a worker to live on common land if his house could be built in one night. This custom was known as *ty unnos*, 'a house built in a single night'.

Houses in Wales are now built of a variety of materials. The traditional stone and slate of the country houses and farms can still be seen, but now brick, concrete and all the other modern building materials are used as well.

Some rural areas of Wales have a particular housing problem. Many houses have been bought by people to use as holiday or second homes. These people can usually pay more than local people can afford, and house prices have risen. This also means that the houses are empty for part of the year, and that the community life of many villages is changing.

10 People, language and culture

Until quite recently there were fears that the Welsh language would die out. Today, however, the Welsh language is in use everywhere. It is spoken at home, at school and at work. Radio and television programmes are broadcast in Welsh, and Welsh is heard on the street and in shops, offices and government departments. It is very much the working language of North Wales, where it was not as threatened as in the south.

Everybody in Wales can speak English, which until the Welsh Language Act of 1967 had been the official language of the country for 400 years. Now government departments produce information and write letters in Welsh and English, and water, gas, electricity and telephone bills are sent out in both languages. Public notices and road signs are in Welsh and English, and jobs are advertised in both languages. From the earliest times there has been a tradition of written Welsh – the language of the poets, the bards and the storytellers.

One hundred years ago most people in Wales spoke Welsh, as they had done for thousands of years. Welsh is one of the oldest European languages. Today, just over half a million people in Wales speak Welsh and there is a growing interest in the language. Schools, colleges and adult education centres hold classes and about 10 000 people in Wales are now learning Welsh. Members of the Welsh Language Society, are

At one time there were fears that Welsh was a dying language, but now it is taught in schools and at Nant Gwrtheyrn, the National Language Centre. The centre was set up in a restored quarrying village on the Lleyn Peninsula in north-west Wales.

pressing for a new Welsh Language Act to acknowledge that Welsh is again the first language of Wales.

Literature

Welsh had already developed as the language of poets and scholars by the end of the sixth century. The earliest surviving poem in Welsh tells the story of a battle in the north-east of what is now England and was then the land of the people called

Gododdin. The poem is called *Y Goddoddyn*.

A wide variety of poetry and prose in Welsh from the twelfth to the fourteenth centuries has echoes of an earlier language. The best-known Welsh prose from that time is the collection of stories called the *Mabinogion*. These are tales of legend and romance, magic and mystery. They are set in the legendary Celtic past, and based on tales that had probably been told for hundreds of years before they were written down.

After Wales was conquered by Edward I in 1282, it was the Welsh bards who helped to keep a sense of Welshness alive. Medieval bards belonged to something like a modern trades union. They were musicians, clerks, historians and secretaries, and they had their own schools with rules and examinations.

Welsh bards travelled all over Wales, entertaining the households of the rich with songs and stories, and writing letters and household lists. Dafydd ap Gwilym was a well-known bard who lived in the fourteenth century. He continued the tradition of praising warriors and making verses to mark important events in the life of those who employed him.

Books in Welsh

The Acts of Union in 1536 and 1543 meant that English became more and more the language of the upper classes in Wales. At that time the rebirth or Renaissance of ideas about painting, architecture and writing was spreading across Europe. Printing had been invented and books were part of every well-to-do household. There was a real danger that Welsh would cease to be used as a language of poetry and scholarship. One court historian, Polydore Vergil, went as far as to write of Welsh history as myth. This was a challenge to Welsh scholars, and in 1546 the first printed book in Welsh appeared.

However, it was the publication of the complete Welsh Bible in 1588, translated by Bishop William Morgan, which saved the language if any one event can be said to have done so. Welsh people heard it read at church throughout the land. Forty years later a Welsh grammar and dictionary were published, and the models for modern Welsh had arrived.

Poetry, ballads, songs, verse dramas, the hymns of William Williams of Pantycelyn (1723-1769) and later, novels, all added to the growth of the language.

The nineteenth century produced a flowering of all kinds of writing by Welsh writers in Welsh and English. The population of the country increased by almost 500 per cent between about 1750 and the end of the nineteenth century, and the number of Welsh people who could read and write also increased. This period saw the revival and growth in importance of the Genedlaethol Eisteddfodd Cymraeg (Welsh National Eisteddfod, or festival of music and arts) as the focus of Welsh cultural life. Many of the works produced for the Eisteddfod were written in the old traditional forms but were now influenced by the religious and moral concerns of the writers.

Modern writers

Twentieth-century writers have produced work in which their use of language shows the influence of earlier writers. Writers such as Kate Roberts, Islwyn Ellis and Jane Edwards have brought everyday language into Welsh writing, giving it a living, changing form.

In the last 50 years writing in Wales in both Welsh and English has seen the emergence of many different and strong voices. It has also seen the growth of publishing inside Wales. Great Welsh poets and writers such as Dylan Thomas (1914-53) were published by English companies. Now the younger voices are coming into print closer to home. The Gomer Press, the University of Wales Press and many small publishing houses are encouraging new writing in Wales.

In Wales today there are many young writers who are aware of their literary history and proud of it. Poets such as R S Thomas write in Welsh and English. Gillian Clarke writes in English, and Tony Conran translates Welsh poetry into English as well as writing his own poetry in English. In the telling of tales and the passing down of poetry the language, customs and humour of the Welsh people have been kept alive.

Gwlad Y Gan - land of song

Eight hundred years ago Gerald of Wales noted that in Wales, '...you will hear as many melodies as you will see mouths...' The Welsh were singing then and they are still.

Whether it is in the formal setting of St David's Hall, Cardiff, or the local chapel, pub or football match, the people of Wales love to sing. The National Eisteddfod represents the highest goal for Welsh singers and musicians and preparing for it has given many people an opportunity they

Each year the National Eisteddfod is held for contestants to compete in literature, music and drama. The poet or bard who composes the best poem in strict Welsh metre wins a carved oak chair and a silver crown is awarded for the best poem in free metre.

would not otherwise have had.

Wales' international reputation in the musical world is upheld by the Welsh National Opera Company and the BBC Welsh Symphony Orchestra. There has also been a Welsh Youth Orchestra since 1945, where young talent is encouraged. In 1947, the Llangollen International Musical Eisteddfod was founded, known throughout the world as a meeting place for singers and dancers. Singers such as Sir Geraint Evans, Dame Gwyneth Jones, and Elizabeth Vaughan are known throughout the world and there are composers such as Daniel Jones and William Mathias. Wales has produced pop stars such as Tom Jones, and the young choirboy Aled Jones. At a more local level folk singers such as Dafydd Iwan, and groups singing in Welsh, such as Maffia Mr Huws, are very popular.

Art and architecture

Wales has produced and still is producing world class painters, architects and artists of other kinds. Painters Gwen John and her brother Augustus, watercolour artist David Jones, Ceri Richards and Kyffin Williams are all well known names. The National Museum of Wales in Cardiff houses a fine collection of Impressionist works, and there are also the Nantgarw, Swansea and Buckley pottery and porcelain collections. Although architect Frank Lloyd Wright's work is mostly in the United States of America, he was Welsh in origin. There is also the astonishing work of Clough Williams Ellis at Portmeirion, where he tried to show that buildings need not ruin a landscape if they are sensitively designed and placed.

This portrait of the famous Welsh poet Dylan Thomas was painted by another famous Welshman, Augustus John.

There are small galleries all over Wales now, showing work of local artists and craft workers as well as holding exhibitions of the work of more famous people. Clwyd County Council have brought part of the collection of the National Portrait Gallery in London to Bodelwyddan Castle in North Wales. Both stately homes and disused industrial sites have been turned into places where the arts flourish. Amongst the best known actors, singers, musicians and playwrights of this century are Richard Burton, Sir Harry Secombe, Siân Phillips, Nerys Hughes, Emlyn Williams, Anthony Hopkins, Meg Wynn Owen, Rachel Roberts, Gwyneth Petty, Angharad Rees – all Welsh. Many of them, and many more, came together in 1988 to record a new production of one of Wales' most famous dramas *Under Milk Wood* by Dylan Thomas.

Arts and crafts

The Welsh Arts Council encourages and gives grants to all forms of the arts in Wales. Individuals as well as companies and groups have benefited from its help.

Theatre and the visual arts are part of the cultural life of Wales. Theatre companies such as Theatr Gwynedd and Theatr Clwyd encourage visiting companies and also produce their own plays. There are small repertory companies such as Theatr Bara Caws which travel around giving shows in village halls. Competitions for new writing, and theatre festivals encourage new Welsh drama, especially amongst young people.

The crafts of Wales have a long history and in recent years there has been a new interest in craft work in Wales. Now there are potteries, jewellery workshops, knitters, weavers, art galleries and metal workers up and down the land.

The new world in Wales shows itself in high technology productions in electronic music, video and film. Cardiff in the south and Caernarfon in the north are becoming centres for work in this field. There are recording companies that produce Welsh language work, and there are many small independent film companies producing films and videos in Welsh.

The British Broadcasting Corporation (BBC) produces programmes in both English and Welsh. Radio Wales and Radio Cymru produce just under half their programmes in Welsh, and there is a Welsh independent television company, Harlech Television. Wales now also has its own Welsh television channel, Sianel 4 Cymru (S4C).

Food

People in Wales today enjoy a basic diet which is similar to that in most developed countries. They eat root and green leaf vegetables such as cabbage, spinach, carrots and potatoes, beans, peas and turnips. Meat, fish, poultry, eggs and cheese, cereals, bread and dairy produce, together with salads and imported vegetables such as peppers or aubergines, provide a reasonably varied diet.

Welsh schoolchildren, however, seem to prefer chips with everything! A 1987 survey showed that children in Wales chose to eat chipped potatoes more often than other children in any of the European Community countries. Health education teachers encourage students to choose a healthier diet for their school meals, but it seems

Local markets sell a variety of fresh local produce such as farm eggs, cheese, cockles and laverbread. Laverbread is made by frying an edible seaweed.

that chips are still the favourite in Wales.

Many people buy their basic groceries such as butter, tea or tinned foods at a large supermarket. Here all kinds of fresh, frozen and packaged or tinned foods can be bought, as well as other household goods such as cleaning materials. Other people shop at smaller, specialist shops such as a local baker or greengrocer.

In many towns in Wales there are weekly markets, where local farm produce is sold. In markets such as Carmarthen, Welshpool or Llangefni people can buy locally grown vegetables, bread and cheeses. Sometimes town markets are held outside and the traders set up covered stalls from which to sell their goods. In other places there may be a Market Hall. Having a market was important for the growth of a town.

More people would visit it to buy and sell, and all kinds of other services such as lawyers or banks set up business there as well.

Wales has always been famous for its Welsh lamb, its potatoes, cheeses and its river salmon. Now farmers in Wales are taking part in the move to grow organic produce. More people want to buy food which has not been grown using pesticides or artificial fertilizers and they want to be sure that poultry and meat comes from animals which have been properly looked after.

Sport

Wales may well be thought of as a musical nation, but it is also very much a sporting country. Rock climbers and hill walkers find some of the best country in the world in the mountains of

Rugby is played enthusiastically throughout Wales, with most towns and villages having their own team. Many young players hope they will be good enough to play for Wales.

Snowdonia and the long distance paths such as Offa's Way and Glyndŵr's Way which stretches across the country and along the borders.

Canoeing and water sports in general are very popular. Outdoor centres at Bala and on the Menai Straits offer courses in all these sports, and white water canoe racing on the Dee River at Llangollen is world class.

Hockey, netball, Association Football, boxing, volleyball, swimming and squash all have their place in the nation's activities. However, rugby became the most popular sport in South Wales in the nineteenth century, and has kept its place. Girls as well as boys play rugby now, but rugby is still part of the tradition of the men of the valleys. They send their young men out into the tough world of rugby to prove themselves and to carry on the pride of Wales. It is still played as an amateur game. The teams play for the game and the honour, not to earn their living.

The Welsh team travels all over the world and also takes part in the Triple Crowns competition, played with France, Scotland, Ireland and England. Such international matches still catch the attention of the nation and are warmly supported. The satisfaction of the crowd when Wales beats England or the good-natured shrug when defeated by the Scotland side perhaps tells that more than just a game is being played out on the rugby field.

Index